JUSTIN CASE SITS WITH ANXIETY

First published in Great Britain in 2025 by Jessica Kingsley Publishers

An imprint of John Murray Press

1

Copyright © Christopher McCurry and Emma Waddington 2025

The right of Christopher McCurry and Emma Waddington to be identified as the Author of the Work has been asserted by them in accordance with the Copyright, Designs and Patents Act 1988.

Front cover image source: Lily Fossett

All rights reserved. No part of this publication may be reproduced, stored in a retrieval system, or transmitted, in any form or by any means without the prior written permission of the publisher, nor be otherwise circulated in any form of binding or cover other than that in which it is published and without a similar condition being imposed on the subsequent purchaser.

A CIP catalogue record for this title is available from the
British Library and the Library of Congress

ISBN 978 1 80501 136 1
eISBN 978 1 80501 137 8

Printed and bound in Great Britain by Bell & Bain Limited

Jessica Kingsley Publishers' policy is to use papers that are natural, renewable and recyclable products and made from wood grown in sustainable forests. The logging and manufacturing processes are expected to conform to the environmental regulations of the country of origin.

Jessica Kingsley Publishers
Carmelite House
50 Victoria Embankment
London EC4Y 0DZ

www.jkp.com

John Murray Press
Part of Hodder & Stoughton Ltd
An Hachette Company

The authorised representative in the EEA is Hachette Ireland,
8 Castlecourt Centre, Dublin 15, D15 XTP3, Ireland (email: info@hbgi.ie)

Justin Case Sits with Anxiety

An Acceptance and Commitment Therapy Workbook for Ages 8-12

Christopher McCurry
& Emma Waddington

Illustrated by Lily Fossett

Jessica Kingsley Publishers
London and Philadelphia

Contents

Acknowledgments — 6

Welcome to This Workbook! — 7

1: What Is Anxiety and Who Is Justin Case? — 11

2: What Matters to You — 20

3: An Old Brain in a New World — 27

4: Justin Meets the Twins — 36

5: Thinking about Anxious Thinking — 42

6: Noticing — 48

7: The Diaper Challenge — 57

8: Allowing, Grounding, and Pivoting — 66

9: Justin Says Goodbye to the Twins and Hello to a Big, New World — 76

For Parents and Caregivers — 80

Acknowledgments

Emma: I want to express my gratitude for the patience and virtue of my husband, Francois, who has allowed me to talk incessantly about my ideas without ever a glimmer of boredom, and my three children, Leo, Nico, and Mia, for being fountains of ideas, laughter, and inspiration for this workbook.

Chris: I am most grateful for the love and support of Sue McCurry: my wife and best friend.

Emma and Chris offer our heartfelt thanks to Jane Evans and all the fine people at Jessica Kingsley Publishers for their hard work and support in making this workbook happen.

Welcome to This Workbook!

Everyone gets scared and worried sometimes. For some people, this may happen quite often. And if you're reading this workbook (and we happen to know you are!), then maybe you're one of the many who struggle with *anxiety*: worried thoughts and icky feelings that show up when life is challenging. Anxiety feels terrible. But, as we'll talk about later, fear and anxiety are *meant* to feel bad in order to get our attention when our brains think we *might* be getting into trouble.

The **BIG** problem with anxiety and worry is that we can get stuck in those awful feelings and thoughts. That's miserable. But the **REALLY BIG** problem is that anxiety can keep us from doing what we want to do or need to do. This workbook will give you a better understanding of how the brain comes up with this anxious stuff, how *normal* that is, and what we can do about it. And, importantly, we will give you strategies for managing anxious situations, "pivoting" away from getting stuck in anxiety, and then moving toward what matters to you.

Living with heart

This workbook does not promise that you will never feel anxious again. No one can promise that. What this workbook is about is *courage*, acting with bravery when you're feeling anxious or scared. The word *courage* comes from an old French word, *corage*, meaning *heart* or *innermost feelings*. We will show you how what matters

most to you, what's in your heart, can help you feel strong when anxious thoughts and feelings show up.

Sometimes we need to pay attention to our brains when they give us a warning. That's when checking in with a trusted adult can be helpful. And, as we'll see with our hero Justin Case, when something truly matters to us, we can find what's in our hearts and take action, letting those worried thoughts and icky feelings come along for the ride.

Words can be powerful

Sometimes just talking about a feeling can invite it to show up. That's the power of words. We'll talk more about that and how you can use the superpower of words to help get unstuck from worry and feeling nervous. We hope you'll share this workbook with people close to you, maybe a parent or friend or teacher. That way, if some of your own anxious thoughts and feelings show up, you can talk about it and get some help or maybe just feel less alone. Everyone you know has a worry story to tell and a story of courage too.

How to use this workbook

It's really very simple. We're inviting you to read a story about our hero, Justin Case. Justin is a boy about your age who has *a lot* of nervous feelings and worries. As you read his story, you can check out the exercises that will help you better understand what anxiety is all about. You'll learn how you can do interesting and important things *even though* you may be feeling anxious. You might want to share what you've learned with the important grown-ups in your life. At the end of this workbook there is a special section just for grown-ups.

Chapter 1
What Is Anxiety and Who Is Justin Case?

What is anxiety?

You probably feel scared or worried sometimes. And you probably don't like it at all. Well, everybody, and we mean *everybody*, thinks and feels this way sometimes. We call scary and worried thoughts and feelings *anxiety*. This workbook is all about what anxiety is and what we can do when it shows up so that you can live your biggest and best life.

So, what do we mean by anxiety?
Here are some of the many words we can use to describe feelings of anxiety and fear. Can you think of any others?

Terrified	Scared	Afraid	Trepidation
Anxious	Alarmed	Nervous	Worried
	Fretful	Pensive	
Apprehensive	Uneasy	Fantods	Concerned

OK, some of these words are pretty strange. Fantods? That's a very old word meaning, "A sudden attack of nervousness or uneasiness." Someone might say, "One look at that roller coaster gave me a case of the *fantods*." That's a fun word to learn, but why do we need all these words for the same thing?

Ah, but are they really all the same? Feeling *scared* is different from feeling *worried*. Scared usually means something bad is happening *right now*, and we often really feel it in our bodies. Worry is almost always a story we're telling ourselves about *the future*; you're imagining something is *going to be* bad.

Words matter

Having different words for our experiences makes the stories we tell more interesting and useful. Let's say you're talking to a friend about a movie you watched. Telling your friend the movie was "funny" is different from telling him it was "hilarious." Telling your mother you're worried about the exam tomorrow is different from telling her you're terrified of the exam.

So, as we talk about anxiety in this workbook, we'll keep coming back to some basic and important ideas. We use "outside words" (language) to *communicate* with others, which is important for getting help when we need it. We use "inside words" (also known as *thinking*) to talk to ourselves. We're always telling ourselves a story about what's going on and how we're doing. And which words we choose for our story matters.

Meet Justin Case

We have our own story to tell you, one we hope you'll find interesting and useful. Our goal in telling you this story is to make your own anxiety stories work better for you. Let us introduce you to a boy named Justin Case. He is 12 years old, and he often feels anxious.

Justin likes to ride his bike, play soccer and video games, do math puzzles, and play with his cat, Sir Pouncelot.

Justin sees himself as very responsible. Keeping his promises is important to him.

Justin is keen to buy himself a new set of tires for his bike. He has been saving for these *forever*. Justin's mom knows about this and has been helping Justin find ways to earn money. Today she had great news for him! His mom's friend and their neighbor, Mrs Amygdala, asked if Justin could come over at 2:00 that afternoon to look after her toddler twins, Blanche and Joy, for a couple of hours while she was in an online work meeting in her home office. Justin felt very grown-up and responsible to be asked. And he was going to be paid for this!

Long before 2:00 Justin started having all sorts of ideas about what could possibly happen in a couple of hours with two-year-old twins, even with their mother right there in the house. What if they started climbing up on something high and fell? What if they started to eat a bug?

What if Justin needed to change a diaper?!

The "what ifs"

That's one of the important things to know about anxiety: it's all about the "what ifs," the "not knowing" what's going to happen. We sometimes call this "not knowing" *uncertainty*. It is the opposite of being "certain" about something. And uncertainty actually happens a lot because no one can predict the future. But we *want* to know. We *need* to know. So when we think about what *might* happen, our imaginations start filling in the blank spaces, the uncertainties. What if *this*? What if *that*?

People are natural story tellers. (Maybe cats are too, but they never share their stories with us.) So we come up with stories about what might happen: later today, tomorrow, next week, five years from now. Sometimes we make up a fun story about the future, and we might call this *daydreaming*: "My birthday is going to be awesome!" Other times, quite often, our minds come up with a worry story: "What if no one comes to my party?" Sometimes thinking about a challenging future situation can help us prepare, but often it just makes us, well… anxious.

Justin prepares

Justin was well prepared. He'd filled his backpack with everything he thought he might need: two water bottles, three protein bars (do toddlers like protein bars?), a Swiss Army knife, a flashlight with extra batteries, his cell phone and charger, a handkerchief, a deck of cards so he could do his new card trick for the twins, and three of his old picture books his mother had saved.

But still, Justin was feeling a lot of excitement and a lot of trepidation. Here's an interesting thought: *excited* feels an awful lot like *scared*, especially in how the body feels, but the story is usually very different. See if this is true for you.

Let's think about the difference between *nervous* and *excited*.

Take a look at this table. (It's called a "table" even though you wouldn't want to eat your supper at it.) It describes two situations Justin is thinking about. We can see how his body is feeling and what he's thinking, or what we're calling "the story."

	THE SITUATION	THE BODY	THE STORY
Justin is feeling *excited*	Playing goalie	Full of energy, light on his feet, focused	"I can do this"
Justin is feeling *excited*	The day he's going to watch the twins	"Butterflies" in his stomach, lots of energy/restless	"This will be fun!" "I can't wait!" "I'm going to earn some spending money!"
Justin is having *worries*	The day he's going to watch the twins	"Butterflies" in his stomach, lots of energy/restless	"This is going to be bad" "I'm going to mess this up and no one will ever trust me again"

Now think of a situation when you've been excited. How was your body feeling then? What was the story you were telling yourself? Write your answers in the table below. Do the same for a situation that made you worried or maybe just *concerned*.

Did you notice that these emotions can *feel* very much the same but have very different *stories* attached to them?

Justin Case Sits with Anxiety

	The situation	The body	The story
I am feeling excited			
I am having worries			

The big takeaways

There are always two parts to our anxiety.

First

First, there is how our bodies are reacting to the situation. Especially with *scared*, it can be a sudden and powerful blast of *feelings*: our bodies tighten up or feel really jumpy or restless, our hearts pound, and there are many other unpleasant feelings. We'll have more to say about why this happens in a little while.

Second

Then there's what we *think*. This is "the story." The story is about how we're *thinking* about our thoughts and our feelings and the situation. And stories matter. Are we *nervous* or are we *terrified*? We'll have more to say about how we can take control of our stories and use them to help ourselves get through anxious situations later.

Now, let's talk about *why* we get anxious. It has a lot to do with what's most important to us.

Chapter 2
What Matters to You

When we care about something or someone, we often have lots of big feelings that come with it. Caring about our friends means that we feel hurt if they're disappointed in us or if they don't want to sit with us at lunch. We care a lot about the safety of ourselves and those we love. We also care about doing a good job, being kind to others, protecting animals. There are lots of things we can care about. And we are all different. Different things are important to each of us. That's what makes humans so interesting and sometimes a little complicated too!

Anxious feelings and worried thoughts are a sure sign that something is important to us. Back to our friend Justin…

Justin is asked to do a babysitting job

As the afternoon of his Big Day got closer, Justin spent a long time thinking of everything that could go wrong.

Thoughts were rushing around in his head. His feelings were a tangled mix of worry and excitement. He tried to push the worry away and just have the excitement, but it wasn't working. So he went to his mom.

Mrs Case was sitting down reading the newspaper. Justin sat down next to her but said nothing at first. Now he was feeling a little embarrassed along with feeling worried. Ugh! Mrs Case could see he was worried.

Justin sighed.

"I hate feeling anxious," he said finally. "No matter how much I prepare, I worry. I can't make it stop. And I hate it. I really hate it," he said.

Mrs Case looked at him with a warm smile. She didn't say anything right away. Justin and she had often talked about his worries. "Ah," she said. "You're having a lot of worries about babysitting the twins. And, yes, no one likes those feelings." She paused, and they sat quietly. Justin still felt anxious, but now he also felt safe at the same time.

Finally, his mother asked, "I'm curious, Justin. What's important to you about doing this job for Mrs Amygdala?"

Justin perked up. "Well, I want to make some money to get some new tires. Man, that would be so cool. And I'd love to help Mrs Amygdala. She's such fun, and I did promise I'd help. I'd hate to let her down. And I love looking after kids. I have fun with them. And I'd also like to feel responsible and grown-up."

"Wow," said Mrs Case, "these sound like lots of important things."

"Yes, I guess they are," replied Justin. "But what about the anxiety?"

Mrs Case put her hand on Justin's shoulder. "Maybe they're both true. You have ideas about what's important *and* you have worry ideas. The worry stuff always seems to show up when we're doing something important."

Justin's mom is absolutely right. Doing important things can make us anxious. Doing things that make us anxious is difficult. Anxiety leads us to want to drop everything and run. We call that an "urge," which we'll talk about in the next chapter. Right now, let's talk about seeing the bigger picture and remember *why* we're doing this difficult thing.

The bigger picture: values and goals

So, we need to spend some time really thinking about why Justin is doing something that's making him feel so uncomfortable. Is it worth it? Sometimes when we face anxiety, nothing feels worth it. Anxiety is such an unpleasant experience, and the thoughts seem so true.

However, here Justin has an opportunity to take a step back and look at the *bigger picture*. Along with his anxious thoughts, he could think of his goals and the things that are important to him. We call these "values": the ideas and actions we think are important. Remembering our values allows us to be courageous and move toward our goals.

JUSTIN'S VALUES	HIS GOALS FOR TODAY
Keeping your promises	Show up (not avoid the job)
Independence	Make some spending money
Being responsible	Do a good job
Kindness	Treat the toddlers well
Courage	Stay "showing up" the whole time

Now let's flip it around. What are some *goals* you have this week? What *values* do these goals come from?

Goals for this week	Values this goal comes from

If it matters to us, we get to worry about it

Let's take a moment to see how what matters to us and anxiety can be connected. Justin cares deeply about being responsible and doing the right thing. That means he worries about not doing a good job. What matters to us can make us anxious.

FOR JUSTIN

| Because being responsible matters to me... | ...I get to worry about doing a good job |

Now, what matters to you and what do you then get to worry about?

Because _____ matters to me...	...I get to worry about _____
Because _____ matters to me...	...I get to worry about _____
Because _____ matters to me...	...I get to worry about _____

When Justin thinks of what is important to him, he can feel the excitement of having new tires and being so proud of his new bike. He can also feel the pride he'd have if he were able to do something as grown-up as babysitting. He likes his neighbor, Mrs Amygdala, and helping her is important to him.

As Justin pondered all this, his anxiety appeared to fade away. "OK, wow, that's cool," he thought. But was it really gone? It was as if Anxiety had said, "I'm so glad you asked," because as soon as he wondered about his worries, there they were, demanding his attention. "Argh, why can't I control my brain?" he thought. Good question. And Justin is not alone in having this struggle with his own brain. Let's look at why that is.

Chapter 3
An Old Brain in a New World

Anxiety is a strong feeling. We are not meant to like or want anxiety. In fact, we evolved to avoid anxiety because it used to mean something *really* bad was going to happen. Our brains are very old. They have the same design as when we were living in caves and running around trying to avoid saber-toothed tigers. Back then, bad things were *very* likely to happen. So when we heard the crackling of a leaf, anxiety was our warning signal: time to hide, fight back (if we could), or run. Nobody was going to hang around to check it out! Those guys got eaten.

Given we have pretty much the same model of brain today, we can expect it to react in the old ways when anxiety shows up. Even though we now have fewer things trying to hurt us, our brains don't quite "know" that.

Our brains: always on alert for danger!

Deep in our brains are two little clumps of nerve cells. These clumps are about the size and shape of almonds, so they're called the *amygdala*, which is Greek for *almond*. They are our security systems, our watch dogs, always looking out for trouble. And these amygdala guys will find trouble and raise the alarm, even when there is nothing to actually worry about.

You may have heard someone talk about the "amygdala hijack." That's when the amygdala alarm system goes off. We sometimes call this the "fight-or-flight" reaction, because when it goes off, we want to fight whatever we think is putting us in danger or run away, fast!

But much of the time, these fight-or-flight reactions are a false alarm. Maybe the smoke detector in your home has gone off when someone has just burned something on the stove. That smoke detector is doing its job, and it doesn't know the difference between a real fire and someone burning the toast. When the amygdala can't tell if this is *real* danger or just *imagined* danger, it (or *they*, as there are two of them) will pull the alarm, and you get hijacked. Better safe than sorry!

When anxiety or fear shows up, our bodies and minds are turned on and turned up. We want to do *something* about it. That pull to want to do something is called an "urge."

Urges

An "urge" is a strong wish or need to do something, usually something that can't wait ("It's *urgent*"). We said that the amygdala hijack is called the fight-or-flight reaction. Those are the two common urges we have. We may have the urge to *fight*: trying to control the situation somehow, maybe not actual *fighting*. Keeping good control of your bicycle when riding on a busy street is smart. Trying to control a teammate because you're thinking they're not playing the game as you'd like may not work so well. Or the urge may be *flight*: to run away or avoid a situation. That might actually be the best thing to do right now. But giving into our controlling, avoiding, and running-away urges too much can make our lives get smaller. We do less of what's important, and that feels awful. Let's talk more about controlling and avoiding, and when that can work.

Let's look at one of Justin's worries and the urge that goes with it.

WORRY	URGE
When I worry about thunderstorms…	…I want to check the weather report every five minutes.

Now, what are some common worries for you, and what are the urges?

Worry	Urge

The cost of avoiding

So, as we mentioned, anxiety makes us want to avoid certain situations. That's its job. And avoiding does work sometimes. It can be very helpful, in fact. Crossing roads with moving traffic *should* make us anxious, and maybe that situation *should* be avoided. But at other times avoidance can be costly.

Let's take a moment to think about the things that we want to avoid and the possible costs in terms of living the lives we want to live.

Things I avoid and the cost

	If I avoid…	The cost is…
Justin	Bungee jumping	None really. Maybe my friends won't think I'm as cool as Brandon, but "whatever'"
Justin	Speaking in front of the class	Poor marks/not gaining confidence
Me		

cont.

	If I avoid…	The cost is…
Me		
Me		

The reality is that avoiding life can make things easier (it can certainly *feel* easier), but it may come at a cost in the long run. Justin could avoid his babysitting job and he would stop feeling anxious. But what would he think and feel after he came off the call to Mrs Amygdala? And when he looked at his bike with the old tires?

Limits of control

We mentioned above that trying to control your poorly playing teammate may not go over so well. Giving in to the urge to control is really frustrating when what we're trying to control is our own thinking and feeling. We might try and stop our thoughts or think of something else.

But many times, trying to control your thinking doesn't work. Especially when the thoughts feel really scary. You just can't reason with those amygdala guys!

If you don't believe us, try this. Don't think about your favorite food. Don't think about it. You're not thinking about it, are you?

The funny thing (actually, it's not that funny) is that the more we try to *not* think about something, the more we tend to think about it. And then what happens is that we work harder at trying not to think about it and… Argh! Thoughts can be very persistent. It's just our brains trying to take care of us. Thanks, but no thanks.

Similarly, we can try and change our feelings. We're thinking, "This anxious feeling is so annoying. And now I'm feeling *annoyed*!" But feelings can't be turned off and on like flipping a switch.

Let's give it a try. Make yourself *love* a food that you just hate. Spinach? Can you do that? Try harder! OK, you probably can't do it. No one can. It's just not under our control. Even if we told you we'd pay you a million dollars if you could love spinach. You might eat it, but you wouldn't *love* it.

So, let's take a moment to think about the things you don't like but try to control. What could be the cost to doing that?

Things I try to control and the cost

	If I try to control...	The cost is...
Justin	The weather	I get frustrated
Justin	How my teammates behave at practice	They get frustrated and annoyed with me
Me		
Me		
Me		

Now, you might think sometimes, "I wish I never felt scared or nervous or worried about anything." We know that sounds awesome, but fear and worry are actually there to help us. We'd be getting ourselves into all kinds of trouble without them.

So, yes, anxiety feels awful (it's trying to get our attention), but the *real* problem with anxiety is that we get "hooked" by anxious thoughts and feelings and they *distract* us. Anxiety wants us to go with our urges to avoid or control at the cost of doing what we need or really want to do.

When we try to avoid our anxious thinking or feelings, we often end up missing out on our important goals and values in life. We need to learn to work with our anxious thoughts instead of focusing on getting rid of them. Ultimately, this is the freedom we really want.

Chapter 4
Justin Meets the Twins

Justin left home with his backpack and started for his neighbor's house. He was having lots of nervous feelings ("Oh, my stomach is NOT happy") and ideas ("What if I need to change a diaper?!?"). On his way to the twins' house, Justin noticed his friend Tristan Glumm bouncing a basketball in front of the Glumm family home across the street.

"Hmm, he looks sad," thought Justin.

"Hey, Tristan, how's it going?" he called.

Tristan looked up. "Hey, Justin. I hope you're coming to my birthday party next week."

"I'll be there," replied Justin enthusiastically.

Tristan sighed, "I guess it's Dolores' party too. You're lucky you're not a twin. We have to share *everything*. My mom says I need to *allow* Dolores to invite whoever she wants. Her dumb friends are going to ruin the party."

"Don't worry," said Justin (thinking, "I'm the worry expert"), "I'll be there, and we'll have a good time together, I promise. Gotta go. I can't be late." He hurried on.

The twins

Justin rang his neighbor's bell. He could feel that the palms of his hands were sweaty and his breathing was faster than usual. His stomach felt a bit rumbly. And all he could think about was how nervous he felt. Ah, fight-or-flight is here! The door opened and Mrs Amygdala greeted him with a warm smile.

"I'm so glad you're here," she said. "Come in. The twins are very excited to see you."

Mrs Amygdala led Justin to a large, brightly lit, and cheerfully decorated room in the house. There were toys and books and child-sized furniture. Justin couldn't see any twins, but in the corner was a blanket that had four feet and giggled. The twins' mother called out, "Justin's here. Come and say hello."

Suddenly, the blanket flew into the air and two voices shouted, "Boo!"

Justin laughed but his heart was beating just a bit faster.

The twins began to run around the room like cars on a racetrack.

"I'll be in my office down the hall," said Mrs Amygdala. "My meeting will last no more than two hours, maybe less. Have fun."

Fun? Justin thought he was going to throw up.

Trying to not have what you already have

As we mentioned in the last chapter, it's very difficult to make yourself feel something you just don't feel. Mmm, spinach. It's the same with trying *not* to think or feel something. Have you ever gotten "the giggles" when it just wasn't OK to have the giggles? Maybe while your teacher was saying something VERY SERIOUS that *sounded* funny. And you tried to not have the giggles and that made you giggle even more. Trying to not have what we have makes us have it even more!

It's the same when we try to talk ourselves out of feeling scared or worried. It just doesn't work very well. We'll talk more about *what to do* when you're feeling anxious in a bit. Right now, we want to mention why it's so hard to think your way out of thinking and feeling this stuff. It's because those amygdala twins (the ones deep in our brains) are like very young children, toddlers, who know only a few words. Mostly, words like "Aaaah!", "Danger!", "Bad!", "Run!", "Freeze!", and "Fight!". They don't listen to reason.

Another important thing that happens during the amygdala hijack is that our attention shrinks down to focus on *the danger*, whether it's real danger or imagined danger. This makes sense: "Hey, you're in danger (so the amygdala are telling us), PAY ATTENTION!" This is helpful if there's a real threat. No daydreaming when you're in danger! But when there's no actual threat, then this shrinking down of our seeing and hearing and thinking means we can miss the important information around us (like we're actually OK) and we don't think of all the possibilities for how to *respond* to the situation. We just *react*.

And there's more

Our stories shrink too. We often think that what we're thinking must be true *because we're thinking it*. Thoughts become *facts* instead of *ideas* we're having. If something is a fact, then there are no other *possibilities*. We think, "This is going to be bad," and that's it. It *is* going to be bad. End of story. We're doomed.

Exercise: Which of these thoughts might be a fact and which might be just an idea?

1. "Video games are dumb."
2. "This is going to be a disaster."
3. "The sun is our closest star."
4. "I'm having anxious feelings right now."
5. "I shouldn't be having anxious feelings right now."

Answers: Facts: 3 and 4. Ideas (maybe we can call them "opinions"): 1, 2, and 5.

OK, maybe it *will* be a disaster, but at the moment you're having that thought, the future is still uncertain and "disaster" is just an *idea*. If we accept these *ideas* that the amygdala give us as *facts*, then we can get stuck. No other possibilities but disaster.

But if we can uncover other possibilities, then we have choices about what we're going to do instead of just going with those *urges* we talked about in the last chapter, the old fight (control) or flight (avoid or escape) reactions.

Recognizing when a thought is a *fact* and when it is an *idea*

How we think (the stories we tell ourselves) is a habit built over time and with lots of practice. It takes some effort and patience *and practice* to build new and better story habits. This is how we start to rewrite our anxiety stories. We start by becoming curious about our thinking; "I'm thinking .... Really? Hmm, I wonder…"

Chapter 5

Thinking about Anxious Thinking

Justin had a lot of anxious thoughts before going to his neighbor's house. And when he got there, he started having new ones! Let's have a closer look into anxious thoughts and see what our minds do when we feel anxious. What kinds of stories do our minds tell us when we are anxious? What do we notice about them?

Justin goes time traveling

The twins were running around the playroom, making quite a racket. "Umm," thought Justin. "This is bound to be interrupting Mrs Amygdala's call. I will need to get them outside to play on the swings."

Then he looked out the window and saw it was drizzling outside. "Well," he thought, "can't go outside."

But he needed to do something. Something responsible. So Justin took a deep breath and thought. It took a moment but then he had an idea. "Raincoats," he thought. "We'll get bundled up and stay warm and dry. This *will* be fun."

But before he could even start looking for raincoats, more thoughts charged into his mind, a barrage of anxious questions: "Is it really a good idea? They will get wet. Could they get sick? Or catch a cold? And it would be my fault. I didn't bring my rain jacket. Why didn't I think of a rain jacket? Why didn't I check the weather report before I left my house?"

His anxiety was rising fast, and he was *time traveling*. Time traveling is when our thinking takes us into the future ("It's going to be bad") or back into the past ("Why didn't I…").

Now, time traveling is not always unpleasant. We can think of the future or the past in ways that are fun and interesting and even helpful. But *anxious* time traveling is very unpleasant and very often not helpful. Our *ideas* about the past or the future become *facts*, and then we get stuck in feeling more anxious and hopeless.

Examples of time traveling

	Fun time traveling	Not-fun time traveling
Justin	Thinking about my friend's birthday party	Imagining failing next week's exams at school
Me		
Me		

Now, thinking about next week's exam might remind us that we need to be studying for it. That would be a helpful action to take. But getting stuck in worrying about the exam *is not* preparing for it.

And even with "fun" time traveling, it's so easy for anxious ideas to creep in. Justin's friend Tristan is having the idea, "What if my friends don't come to my party?" Not fun. Not helpful. But when that stuff just shows up, we might say, "Hmm. That's an interesting idea. I wonder if it's true?"

The best or the worst

Think about when you do some future time traveling. Maybe you're imagining an upcoming holiday or event or challenging situation. It's easy (and fun) to imagine the *best* possible outcome.

For example, Justin might think, "I'm going to score two goals at the game and be the hero." But as so often happens, we can quickly imagine the *worst* possible outcome: "I'm going to miss all my shots and they'll blame me for losing the game and I'll need to change my name and move to another country." Yes, the amygdala can get pretty dramatic!

What's difficult for us to imagine is the "messy middle": that mix of positive and negative that is so often what life gives us. Maybe, when the time came, Justin didn't score two goals, but he played well, helped his team, and it certainly wasn't a disaster. The amygdala might find that boring, but it's probably closer to what will really happen.

Think of a recent situation that you thought about a lot. What were the "best" and the "worst" ideas you had about that situation before it happened. What actually happened?

Justin Case Sits with Anxiety

Situation	The worst that I imagined	The best that I imagined	What actually happened

We often get hooked by our scariest thoughts exactly because they are scary. However, getting hooked by our stories can stop us from doing the very things that we want to do. Getting hooked by disaster ideas can keep us from doing our best or even trying at all. That makes our lives smaller.

How do we get unhooked from unhelpful stories? It starts with just *noticing* them for what they are: *stories*.

Chapter 6
Noticing

Justin decided against going outside but had a new idea: "I'll show the twins my new card trick." He started looking through his pack to find the cards. "Ah, found them."

But when he looked up, the twins were gone. "Oh, no," he thought (with some feelings of *terror*), "I've lost them already."

He looked all around the room but could not see them anywhere. "Calm down!" he told himself. "They must be here somewhere."

So Justin took a deep breath, closed his eyes, and listened. As he slowly breathed out, he noticed giggling coming from one corner of the room. He opened his eyes and noticed that the twins' blanket was piled up there and moving slightly.

"The blanket again," Justin thought. "I guess two-year-olds don't have much imagination."

"Oh, no," he said out loud. "What am I going to do? I've lost Blanche and Joy!" The blanket started to laugh.

Noticing

Here's an example of a famous illusion called Rubin's Vase. What do you see?

If you focus on (notice) the white part, then you're probably seeing the "vase" or goblet. If you notice the black part, then you're probably seeing the profiles of two people facing each other. Weird, huh? Both images are there. But which we see, the vase or the faces, depends on which we're paying attention to, which we're *noticing*.

The first step in getting unhooked from anxious thinking and feeling and the urges is to simply notice and label what's showing up in your mind at the moment. "Wait a minute," we can hear Justin say. "How can I get unhooked if I'm *focusing* on what I'm thinking and feeling?!"

Good question. Noticing is different from focusing on, *and getting pulled into*, our anxious thoughts and feelings and the stories they invite us to create. This is hard to describe, but we know you will *feel* the difference with practice.

When we're *noticing*, we're "stepping back" a bit from what's going on. Saying, "I noticed the clouds," is different from saying, "I saw the clouds." It's just a little more curious, a little more, "Hmm, that's interesting," even when feelings and ideas are running hot.

Like switching from the vase to the faces, we can *pivot*

our attention from anxious thoughts and feelings to our values and goals. You might notice (there it is again) that the "vase" doesn't need to go away in order to notice the "faces." Or the other way around. In the same way (and this is important), our anxious thoughts and feelings don't need to go away in order to notice we're hooked by them and to then pivot our attention to what would be helpful in that situation. We'll describe pivoting in a bit. And we can, we must, pivot *even though* the anxious thoughts and feelings are still hanging around.

Noticing can help you be *curious* about strong, challenging emotions instead of struggling with them: "Oh, I'm thinking *that* again." Noticing helps us see important differences, as we did with the words we use for anxiety. For example, are we *scared* or are we *nervous*? Maybe we're just a bit *uneasy*. These differences create different stories.

Toddlers and card tricks

The twins weren't interested in Justin's card trick, but they did enjoy spreading the cards all over the floor.

"No, no, no," Justin told them. But they ignored him. He noticed that you can't argue with two-year-olds or even have much control over them.

He had a new thought: "As long as they're not getting hurt, it is OK to just let them have fun."

He started to relax a bit and began to focus on the twins instead of focusing on his anxious feelings. He became aware that he could actually start to tell the twins apart: Blanche's face was a bit paler than Joy's, and when Joy smiled, a dimple appeared in her right cheek.

The skill of *noticing*

We can "train up" our noticing as a helpful tool for getting unhooked from unhelpful thoughts and feelings. Noticing is a *skill*. We're guessing you already have many skills. You probably don't even think much about some of them anymore, like tying your shoes or riding a bicycle. But every skill you have, whether it's playing the piano or dribbling a soccer ball, you had to learn and practice to get *skilful*.

Learning a skill and practicing it can feel awkward, even boring. But there's no way around practicing if we want to get better at something. Are we starting to sound like your coach?

We practice with *intention*. Doing something "with intention" means we're doing something on purpose: it's something we mean to do. When we do something with intention, we're giving it our full attention; we're *really* doing it.

What can we notice with intention?

Anything, really: an itch on your nose, the sound of rain on the roof, even how twins can look different. We can notice our anxious thoughts and feelings *and how they're trying to hook us*. We can notice and label our *urges*. For example, when Justin feels anxious, he has the urge to try and control the situation. If that doesn't work, he has the urge to turn and run. Noticing these urges as soon as they show up can help him come up with new ideas about what to do.

Breathing

Breathing is something we're all doing all the time. I'm breathing right now, and so are you. You probably breathe in and out 20 to 30 times each minute. Maybe more when you're running or excited. Maybe fewer when you're relaxed or asleep. But we're talking 30 to 40 *thousand* breaths per day. All day. All night. Awake and asleep. And most of the time, we're not even aware we're doing it!

But being aware of our breathing, at least some of the time, can be helpful because *how* we breathe matters. It can have a powerful effect on our thoughts and feelings. And, importantly, *it's something we can control*, even when we can't control the anxious thoughts and feelings that just show up. We can use breathing to help us feel grounded (we'll talk about getting *grounded* in a bit). We can use our breathing to practice noticing and focusing.

Exercise: Noticing practice: cool and warm, in and out

Take a minute to just breathe in and out of your nose, naturally, not too fast or too slow. Notice something: when you breathe in through your nose, does the air coming in feel a bit cool and tingly against the skin surrounding your nostrils?

And when you breathe out, again through your nose, do you notice that the air is now warmer (it was warmed up inside your body for those few seconds) and now you can barely feel it leaving your nose? Can you notice that very small but clear difference: cool and tingly going in, warm and barely felt coming out? That simple action is training your brain's noticing skill.

Exercise: Focusing (and *re*-focusing) practice

Start focusing on your breathing, naturally, in and out. Now start counting your breaths: in and out is one, in and out again is two, and so on up to ten. When you get to ten, start over at one on the next breath.

Here's the thing: *You're going to get distracted and lose count.* Everyone does. And that's an *opportunity* to notice you've lost count and to get back on track. You're not just noticing your breaths; you're noticing *not noticing* them!

Exercise: Calming breath practice

You may have heard of this one: Smell the flower, blow out the candles. It's very simple. Breathe in through your nose, just like you're smelling a lovely flower. A nice, long, relaxed breath in.

Then blow out the candles by breathing out through your mouth. Make it a *looong* breath out. Make sure you get all the candles. Repeat three times.

More skills to learn and practice and use

You can use these breathing exercises to build your noticing and focusing skills. In the final chapter of this workbook there's a list of helpful books. Two of these books, *Sitting Still Like a Frog* and *Child's Mind*, can help you and the grown-ups in your life learn more about noticing and many other cool skills.

When anxiety does show up, you'll be ready to get unstuck and not just go with your urges. You'll be able to just notice your anxious thoughts and feelings, allow them to be there (since they're already there), and pivot your focus to what matters. What do we mean by *allowing* anxiety to be there? We'll talk about that in the next chapter as Justin deals with a very smelly situation.

Chapter 7
The Diaper Challenge

Justin was feeling more settled. He watched the twins laugh and giggle as they threw the cards around the room. "They're having so much fun! Life is simple for two-year-olds," he thought.

Suddenly, he noticed something rather pungent in the air. Justin turned toward the twins. They were still running around, and as Blanche moved closer, Justin had to turn his head away as the sour smell crawled up his nose. "It's coming from her," he thought. Oh no. *A dirty diaper*. This was the *last* thing he wanted to deal with. And it smelt like a *big* one.

Justin felt disgusted. The smell was a ghastly mix of rotten eggs and something else. He suddenly felt sick. "Um, let me look away and think of the camping trip next week instead or anything else," he thought. But he couldn't time travel away from that smell.

Justin was going to have to tackle this. It's part of the job, part of being responsible. His mother had showed him how to change a diaper using one of his sister's dolls. But doing it alone was the real thing! He needed to accept the situation and deal with it whether he wanted to or not. "I'll breathe through my mouth," he thought, as he took a great big inhale.

Willingness

Justin needing to accept the situation didn't mean he had to like it. When we talk about *acceptance* or being *willing* to do something, we don't mean, "I'm happy this is happening," or "I agree with this." Justin was certainly not happy about having to change Blanche's diaper!

However, accepting a situation as it is can be very helpful. We can look at acceptance as simply noticing what is happening in this moment and *allowing* it to be there, then adapting to the situation in a helpful way. This is very different from struggling with what is happening and working hard to make it disappear. It is also very different to *wanting* it to happen. We can have *willingness* without *wantingness* (a word we just made up, but you get the idea). So, there are times where we have to do things we don't *want* to do because it helps us get to the valued goals that matter to us. Willingness is a powerful tool for reaching our goals.

Wantingness and willingness

Here are a couple of situations where Justin does not *want* to do something, but because of his values and goals, he is *willing* to do it. Think of some situations where this might be true for you.

Justin Case Sits with Anxiety

	Value or goal	I don't want to...	I'm willing to...
Justin	To be responsible	Change the diaper	Change the diaper
Justin	To be a good teammate	Go to practice	Go to practice
Me			
Me			

Pretty simple, huh? But not always easy to do. That's OK. *Everyone* you know struggles with this.

Thoughts and feelings like clouds in the sky

When we get hooked on anxious thoughts and feelings and the urges that come with them, we may lose sight of our values, of what is important in the moment. What's important to us is always there, even when strong thoughts and feelings push their way to the fronts of our minds. Think of it like the sky.

Have you ever been on an airplane that took off on a cloudy day? You get on the plane with this soggy, grey, cloud-stuffed sky above you. Then the plane takes off and climbs higher and higher until, suddenly, it breaks through the clouds and there's brilliant sun and blue sky that you forgot was there. It's such a surprise that it makes you laugh.

Even on the cloudiest day, the sky is still there. Even when we're feeling really stuck in and hooked by anxious thoughts and feelings, our values and the goals they give us are there for us to remember and connect with.

> ### Exercise: The sky and the clouds
>
> Take a crayon and paper and draw a sky. Add some clouds. Go ahead and draw lots of clouds. Inside them, write some of your difficult thoughts and feelings. Notice how you don't have to believe or react to all these thoughts. You can just let them come and go like clouds in the sky. For example, you can be *disappointed* in the weather ("Oh, no! It's *raining*") and still allow it to be the way it is and adjust your plans for the day.
>
> Know that you're more than your thoughts and feelings. They come and go, like clouds. You are the sky!

Justin had a choice to make. He *could* avoid changing Blanche's diaper. But this would mean that he wasn't being responsible and taking good care of the twins. This is usually the choice before us. We can avoid what we don't want, *and* it often comes at a cost. We talked about *the cost* of avoiding things in Chapter 3. Maybe the cost is immediate: that diaper is not going to get *unstinky*; it's only going to get worse. Or the cost may just be a lost opportunity to learn and grow.

Two sides of the same coin

Have you heard of the saying, "Two sides of the same coin"? It means that often there's two sides, or two stories, to every situation. Usually, one story is positive ("I was recognized for my soccer skills") and there's a story that's not so positive ("Now I must *really* practice"). These are each two sides of the same coin; for example, getting picked for the elite team.

One side of the coin has the "good stuff," the stuff we want. On the other side we have the "challenging stuff," the stuff we need to be willing to have or to do. Notice that we said, the "challenging stuff," not the "bad stuff." It's just stuff we need to do to live the life we want to have.

For Justin, on one side of the coin, there are his values of being responsible and kind, the good stuff he wants. On the other side, we find the challenging stuff; for example, dealing with the stinky diaper.

Here's what that might look like as two sides of the same coin.

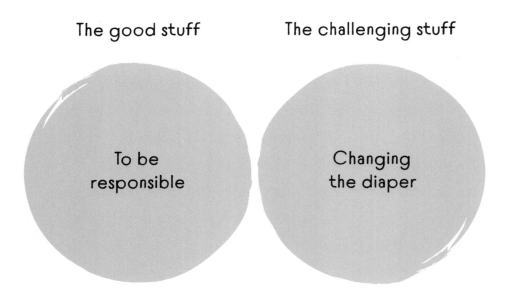

If Justin says, "I'm not willing to change this diaper." Well, then he's tossing away "being responsible" and "being kind" too. They are two sides of the same coin.

Now, going back to your values, what might be on the two sides of one of *your* coins as you think about a challenging situation that's coming up? This could be an important exam at school or something to do with a friend or a family member. Put your values and goals on one side and challenging stuff on the other.

If you like, you can cut out a circle of paper and make a "coin" that you can keep someplace, such as on your desk at home or on your bedroom dresser, as a reminder of what's

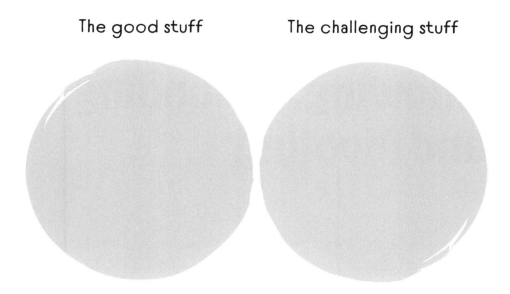

good as well as the challenging stuff you need to make room for.

So, when anxiety shows up, we may try to get rid of it by avoiding what is making us anxious or trying to control the situation in ways that aren't helpful. We may feel better right away, and for a little while, but we miss out on things and we don't learn that we are way more capable than we realize. We've mentioned this idea of the *pivot*: changing our focus from the vase to the faces, from being stuck to "being willing." Let's talk about how that's done.

Chapter 8

Allowing, Grounding, and Pivoting

Justin was faced with the disgusting but important task of changing Blanche's diaper. Or maybe it's Joy. Justin was so focused on his disgust and anxiety that he had lost the ability to notice which twin he was looking at. To get unstuck and do the job, Justin needed to *allow* the anxious thoughts and feelings to just be there, because they were already there. Fighting what you're already feeling and thinking just takes you away from living your best life.

As we've said, the problem with anxiety is that it is a *distraction*. This chapter will provide several exercises for getting unhooked from anxiety. We talked about "noticing" in Chapter 6. That's the starting point. Now we're going to talk about "allowing," getting settled or "grounded," and then "pivoting" into willingness.

Let's think about what allowing might look like. Maybe you've found yourself in this very situation.

A lesson in allowing: the crowded chair

Imagine you're in your house, sitting alone in a big comfy chair. You're playing a favorite video game. Ah, it's great. But then your little brother comes into the room. Maybe it's your cousin. They sit on the chair next to you and watch what you're doing. You're feeling a little annoyed, but you go back to focusing on your game. Then more brothers or sisters or cousins start coming into the room *and joining you on the chair*! It's now gotten quite crowded and you're feeling quite distracted from your game. What do you do?

Well, you can fuss at the intruders, elbow or bump the ones on either side. You could quit the game. Maybe go get help from an adult. But then you're no longer playing your game.

But maybe you could *allow* them to be there. Not happily, of course. But allowing them to be there, since they're already there, would *allow you* to focus on your game or show or whatever you were doing before they all showed up.

Now, that doesn't mean you can't stand up for yourself. Not at all. Sometimes, though, we need to be willing to have, to make room for, to sit with, certain thoughts and feelings (or people) that have shown up so that we can

67

stay focused on what we want. Justin's friend Tristan will need to *allow* his sister's friends to be at *their* party and do his best to stay focused on having a good time. Justin is learning to *sit with* his anxiety. Now that he's made room for these ideas and feelings (and smells), Justin needs to get *grounded*. Then he can *pivot* toward his goal.

Grounding

Grounding, or getting grounded, means feeling like you're really here, right now. It's the opposite of time traveling or being so caught up in your thinking that you're unaware of what's going on around you. It's hard to describe it, but we know when we feel it.

Justin loves soccer. He especially likes to play goalie. He knows he plays best when his "head is in the game." Justin knows from experience that if he lets his mind wander, whether it's a pleasant daydream or a worry about the future ("I'm going to let them score and everyone will be angry with me"), he can miss the ball coming his way. Exactly what he doesn't want! Justin needs to be right there, feeling the solid turf beneath his feet while not feeling "stuck" to the earth. He needs to be focused on all the movement in front of him, ready to spring in any direction.

We can get ourselves "grounded" even when a situation makes us feel overwhelmed, anxious, or unsure of what to do. There are many techniques we can use to get grounded. We will describe a few here. The goal is to get your focus in the "just right" zone: not too small ("This diaper is disgusting!") and not too big ("I can't do this!"). You want to be in the here and now so that you can connect with what's important and take action toward your valued goal. Grounding won't make negative feelings and ideas go away. But it will help you when anxious stuff shows up and starts to pull you away from doing what matters. It's like an anchor on a boat; they both keep us from drifting away.

Two quick and easy ways to get grounded

FIND YOUR FEET: We can get stuck in our heads, thinking anxious thoughts and getting distracted from what we need to do. Remembering that you have feet, putting your attention on them, and feeling the pressure of the bottoms of your feet against the floor or whatever surface they're on can help get you feeling more settled, more grounded. Try it right now!

BREATHE: We talked about breathing in Chapter 6. We can start to get grounded, to feel more secure and solid,

> by just taking two or three breaths *with intention*. We also mentioned this word "intention" in Chapter 6. It's when we're really focused on what we're doing. We're doing it with purpose. Slow, steady, intentional breathing actually gets the amygdala guys to start calming down. It's science!

Pivoting

When we "pivot," we're making a move to face in a new direction, usually without moving from where we're standing. Justin does this when he's goalie in soccer, standing in one place in the box but moving his head, and sometimes his shoulders, in the direction of the action. He's pivoting.

Breathing pivot
Focusing on breathing, slowly and with intention, can do that for us. We pivot our attention away from anxiety and toward our breathing. Remember the vase/faces illusion, also from Chapter 6. All that anxious stuff will probably still be there, but it won't be in your face so much. Or vase! From focusing on your breathing, we can then pivot to other helpful moves, such as getting a diaper changed or just walking out the door to head to school.

Two more ways to pivot

FIND YOUR HANDS: When you're up in your head, caught up in a lot of anxious ideas, find your hands. They're close by. Ah, there they are! And now that you've found them, put them to work doing whatever it is you could or should be doing *right now*. This will swing your attention back out here into the here and now and get you active instead of stuck in the mental muck.

Dropping Anchor: a grounding and pivoting exercise

Dropping Anchor is an exercise you can do when you're feeling anxious and overwhelmed and need to get grounded. It is an *acronym*. An acronym is a word where each of the letters of that word are the first letter of another word. It's a cool way of remembering things. The acronym for Dropping Anchor is ACE.*

A: Acknowledge your inner experience

By "acknowledge," we mean notice, name, and allow what your mind is coming up with in that moment. In this first

---

* We want to thank Dr Russ Harris (2009) for coming up with Dropping Anchor. Harris, R. (2009) *ACT Made Simple*. Oakland, CA: New Harbinger Publications.

step, we take a curious look at our thoughts, feelings, and urges in the moment. Justin is noticing that he's having the thought that this diaper changing is disgusting, that he's feeling a bit sick to his stomach, and that he has the strong urge to call the twins' mother to come and take care of this mess.

C: Come back into your body
Often, when we're feeling anxious, we're way "up in our heads" and we lose touch with our bodies. Here's where we get grounded. Justin feels his feet on the floor, he relaxes his shoulders (he noticed they were almost touching his ears), and he becomes more aware of his hands ("be gentle"). He does wish that his body, just for those minutes, did not include *a nose*.

E: Engage the world
This is where we pivot. We bring our attention back to what's going on out here in the world ("Oh, that's right. I'm in the middle of a diaper change. Best to *finish* it.") instead of being distracted by anxious feelings and ideas. Now, the "what's going on" may not be pleasant right now. Dropping Anchor is not going to make Justin *love* changing diapers! And, if Justin is going to be careful and efficient and successful in changing the diaper, he needs to *engage*

that task: to pivot to being present and focused and moving in a valued direction.

Two more grounding and pivoting acronyms

BOLD:*

Breathe.

Observe what you're thinking and feeling.

Listen to your values.

Decide what to do.

BEAR:**

Breathe.

Expand (your thinking if it's too "the worst" or "I can't" and there are other signs you're stuck).

Act (take action).

Remember (how well did that action work for you?).

---

*   Another "thank you." This one is to Dr Louise Hayes for BOLD (Ciarrochi, Hayes, and Bailey, 2012). Ciarrochi, J., Hayes, L., and Bailey, A. (2012) *Get Out of Your Mind and Into Our Life for Teens*. Oakland, CA: New Harbinger Publications.
** We came up with this one on our own!

Justin does BOLD

1. He **breathes** (through his mouth!).
2. He **observes**, or *notices*, what he's thinking ("This is disgusting" and "I can't stand this").
3. He **listens** to his values: "Hey," they tell him, "be responsible, be brave!"
4. He **decides** to focus on getting the diaper changed, quickly but carefully.

"It's OK," Justin said gently. "We'll get this done right away." He remembered what his mother had taught him and smoothly got the diaper away, the toddler cleaned up, and the new diaper in place. He let out a long sigh of relief. The child smiled at him. Then he saw the dimple. It was Joy!

Your turn (no, we're not going to have you change a diaper)

Can you think of some situations over the next week or so where you might get stuck in some anxious thoughts and feelings? How could you use one of these tools?

Allowing, Grounding, and Pivoting

Justin's challenging situation	His difficult thoughts and feelings	What he needs to pivot toward	A tool he could use
Speaking in front of his class	"I'm going to totally mess this up"	Just giving the talk I've been practicing	Dropping Anchor
Your challenging situation	Your difficult thoughts and feelings	What you need to pivot toward	A tool you could use

75

Chapter 9
Justin Says Goodbye to the Twins and Hello to a Big, New World

It's been a busy afternoon for Justin. He has had lots of thoughts and ideas about how things could go wrong. He had prepared himself for all sorts of problems. And that's just what anxiety does; it wants us to be prepared for all the possible catastrophes that could happen – just in case. Our minds travel with anxiety, mostly into the future and always into the worst-case scenarios. This is what our minds were built to do many, many years ago. It's kept us safe, certainly. But also, unhappy and distracted sometimes.

Despite everything he did to prepare himself for the situation, Justin still had lots of anxiety. He also noticed that the more he tried to control or get away from his anxiety, the stronger his anxiety got.

Justin learned that he could allow and make room for some

challenging feelings and ideas and still focus on his values and goals. Focusing on his goals and values means he gets to live a life that's full of color and things that matter to him. In the story, we saw how Justin got to be responsible, take good care of the twins, and earn himself some money for his new tires. Justin also cares a lot for Mrs Amygdala and was keen to help her. He is ready to take on more challenges and learn and grow from those experiences (the "remember" part of BEAR).

A key lesson is that we do best when we give up the struggle of trying to control or avoid important situations if doing so prevents us from living our values and getting to our goals.

Justin stood at the open front door. The world beyond it seemed bright and full of possibilities. Mrs Amygdala thanked him for being so helpful, paid him (yes!), and said she hoped she could count on him again. She put a hand on his shoulder and said, "I know this was your first time looking after young ones on your own." Mrs Amygdala laughed and said, "I still remember how nervous I was my first time and that was many years ago. But that's how we grow, by getting out of our comfort zone." Suddenly, the twins came running up and each grabbed one of Justin's legs in a fierce hug. They laughed and, just as quickly, were gone again. Justin felt his heart grow bigger.

A final metaphor

Imagine you want to build a house of bricks. You have a great pile of bricks, and you start going through the pile selecting the bricks you want to build with. With your beautiful new house in mind, you start by only selecting the perfect bricks, the ones with no blemishes or irregularities and with just the right color. But you quickly find that most of the bricks are not perfect. There's something about many of them in the pile that you find unappealing, and you toss them aside. But then you realize that a house made of only perfect bricks will be quite small.

A rather small house is certainly an option. But if you want a house that is spacious and can accommodate lots of friends and activities and possibilities, you're going to need some, maybe many, of the less-than-perfect bricks.

If we work at only having pleasant thoughts and feelings, we will often be frustrated (not a pleasant feeling) and we will be missing out on so much that life has to offer. A full life means a life full of feelings of many different types, especially the ones we do like!

And we say goodbye

We hope you've enjoyed Justin's story, and we hope you've learned some useful things. Anxiety is not fun, but it comes from our caring about others and about ourselves. We can do great things when we make room for challenging feelings and ideas, remember our values, and move toward our goals. We wish you all the best as you continue to write your own story of courage!

For Parents and Caregivers

In this chapter, we would like to describe some simple steps by which you, the important grown-up, can support the strategies and skills we've presented. At the end of this chapter, we list several books for further reading. We'll start with a brief description of the therapy this workbook is grounded in.

Acceptance and commitment therapy

This workbook, and the ideas and the exercises in it, are based on *acceptance and commitment therapy,* often shortened to ACT, said as one word and not a-c-t. ACT came out of cognitive behavioral therapy, or CBT, which you may have heard of. Traditional CBT emphasizes changing ("restructuring") one's anxious thoughts and feelings, largely through rationalization. For example, we might ask ourselves, "How likely is it that I'll completely fail this exam?" We might assure ourselves that *complete* failure is unlikely and then try to *push out* anxiety with some confident self-talk. And this may work from time to time or for a little while. But most people discover that anxious thoughts and feelings don't just bow down to rational arguments. The brain is great at the "Yes, but..." game.

Backed by a large body of research, ACT's approach instead recognizes that difficult thoughts and feelings, such as those we have with anxiety, are often a natural and expectable part of living an interesting and vital life. That's the *acceptance* part of ACT. Instead of getting caught up in trying to talk ourselves out of what we're thinking and feeling, ACT reminds us that we're anxious largely because *we care*, because what we're doing matters to us. And the best response to anxiety is often to reconnect with our values and goals and then pivot toward those goals, taking steps, perhaps small ones, in that direction. That's the *commitment* part.

What you can do

You can support your child in their anxious situations by following these three steps: validate, pivot, move.

STEP 1: Validate (label) your child's thoughts and feelings with useful language

Your child's anxious behavior (e.g., balking at readying for school) is communicating their distress to you. Validation says, "Message received." We like "Ah..." statements: "Ah, you're feeling _____ now." Fill in the blank with whatever word provides an accurate and perhaps nuanced understanding of what they're feeling in the moment. As we described in Chapter 1, there are important, if subtle, differences amongst feeling words; for example, "nervous" versus "terrified."

You can reflect back, or validate, anxious thoughts: "Ah, you're having one of those _____ *ideas* right now." We like using the word "idea" because, as we mentioned, when people are stressed, they tend to regard their thoughts as facts: "It *will* be a disaster." Calling this an "idea" sidesteps arguing with the child or trying to get them to change their thinking, but it does serve to identify this mental activity as something other than a true fact.

Two important points. First, you don't need to agree that this is something your child *should* be anxious about. You're just saying, "I get you right now." Second, validation won't turn off your child's anxious thoughts, feelings, and behaviors like flipping a switch. But until a person *feels heard* and can start reworking their story (e.g., "nervous" for "scared"), they can remain stuck and unable to move forward.

STEP 2: Change the focus of attention (pivot)

Anxiety takes us out of the present and away from our goals. After validation of your child's feelings and ideas, you can gently redirect them to the present moment. This could be as simple as asking the child to look at you: "Look at me, please. Thank you." You might remind your child to try the BOLD or BEAR acronym strategies in the moment.

Taking three mindful breaths can be helpful to draw attention away from anxious thoughts and feelings and allow for a pivot. However, many children (and adults too!) will resist, or take offense, if you say, "Just take some deep breaths." Validating first, helping your child "feel heard," can reduce resistance to your suggestions.

STEP 3: Orient and move toward valued goals

After validation, you can reorient your child to place, time, and task: "OK, it's ten minutes to 8:00. You're in the kitchen. Your shoes are in your bedroom. I need you to go there, get them, and bring them to the bench by the front door." Or: "Let's look at the list of homework questions and pick *one* to start with. I will be back in five minutes to see how you're doing."

Parent anxiety

What's more anxiety-provoking than being a parent?! When our children are anxious or distressed in some way, as parents, we are necessarily pulled into the story, and we get to think and feel our own predictable set of emotions and ideas. Our thinking can become either too small or too big. We too can get very black-and-white, all-or-none: "Why does he *always* do this?" Your own practicing and modeling of the strategies and skills in this workbook can help. You can *notice and label* your own thoughts and feelings in the moment and *allow* them to be there. You can *pivot* your attention toward potential coping or problem-solving strategies based on *your* valued goals: "I need to be patient right now." This helps you stay in command of the situation and models for your child how they might cope as well.

Patience and practice

We're talking about developing a new set of skills, building new habits, for your child *and for you*. These new responses to your child's anxiety, and your own thoughts and feelings, may feel awkward at first. But with diligent practice, these skills will become smoother, more natural, and more automatic. Be patient with your child and with yourself. Struggling with anxiety is among the most deeply human things we do.

But so too is showing compassion and love. Employing healthy doses of the latter, especially self-compassion, will see you through this journey.

Further reading

Coyne, L. W. and Murrell, A. R. (2009) *The Joy of Parenting*. Oakland, CA: New Harbinger Publications.

Kastner, L. S. (2013) *Wise Minded Parenting*. Seattle, WA: ParentMap.

McCurry, C. (2009) *Parenting Your Anxious Child with Mindfulness and Acceptance*. Oakland, CA: New Harbinger Publications.

Race, K. (2013) *Mindful Parenting*. New York: St. Martin's Griffin.

Schonbrun, Y. (2022) *Work Parent Thrive*. Boulder, CO: Shambhala.

Snel, E. (2013) *Sitting Still Like a Frog*. Boston, MA: Shambhala.

Willard, C. (2010) *Child's Mind: Mindfulness Practices to Help Our Children Be More Focused, Calm, and Relaxed*. Berkeley, CA: Parallax Press.

The Story Continues!

Want to find out more about Justin's friend Tristan Glumm and his twin sister Dolores or discover how Max Cross navigates through anger?

Read the other books in the series:

The Glumm Twins Unhook from Sadness

An Acceptance and Commitment Therapy Workbook for Ages 8–12

Christopher McCurry and Emma Waddington

ISBN 978 1 80501 138 5
eISBN 978 1 80501 139 2

Max Cross Gets Unstuck from Anger

An Acceptance and Commitment Therapy Workbook for Ages 8–12

Christopher McCurry and Emma Waddington

ISBN 978 1 80501 140 8
eISBN 978 1 80501 141 5

Read More Books from JKP!

Notes